THE LANGUAGE
OF THE AMERICAN SOUTH

THE LANGUAGE

OF THE

AMERICAN SOUTH

CLEANTH BROOKS

MERCER UNIVERSITY
LAMAR MEMORIAL LECTURES
No. 28

THE UNIVERSITY OF GEORGIA PRESS

ATHENS

© 1985 by the University of Georgia Press
Athens, Georgia 30602

Set in 11 on 14 pt. Linotron 202 Baskerville

The paper in this book meets the guidelines for
permanence and durability of the Committee on
Production Guidelines for Book Longevity of the
Council on Library Resources.

Printed in the United States of America

89 88 87 86 85   5   4   3   2   1

Library of Congress Cataloging in Publication Data

Brooks, Cleanth, 1906–
The language of the American South.

(Lamar memorial lectures ; no. 28)
1. American literature—Southern States—History and
criticism—Addresses, essays, lectures. 2. English
language—Southern States—Addresses, essays, lectures.
3. Southern States in literature—Addresses, essays,
lectures.   4. English language—Style—Addresses, essays,
lectures.   I. Title. II. Series.
PS261.B76 1985   810'.9'975   84-28065
ISBN 0-8203-0782-3 (alk. paper)

To Robert and Ruth Heilman

Contents

Foreword

MR. BROOKS DECLARES THE PURPOSE OF *The Language of the American South* very clearly: "I mean in these lectures to pay special tribute to the language itself." It is a rich language, he says, and it has been richly used. After first suggesting, in a recurrence to some of the interests at the beginning of his distinguished career, that the distinctiveness of much Southern vocabulary and pronunciations is traceable to England rather than to "distortion," he turns to examples of the use of this distinctive Southern language in writers of the nineteenth and twentieth centuries.

In the course of this survey he brings the reader considerable instruction and delight as he offers the evidence for his assertion that even the formal diction of Southern writers is strengthened by "their knowledge of, and rapport with, the language spoken by the unlettered" and that the character of the Southern language has survived the transition from Old to New South.

There was much to appreciate not only in the lectures, delivered by Professor Brooks at Mercer in October 1984, but also in the lecturer. Mr. Brooks, a principal figure of twentieth-century criticism, author of *The Well-Wrought Urn* and *William Faulkner: The Yoknapatawpha Country*, coauthor of *Understanding Poetry* and *Modern Rhetoric*, was by strictest and warmest definition a gentleman, quick and cordial in response to everyone who approached, gracious at every moment. And his own diction was a joy to hear, a worthy vehicle for his ringing peroration, toward the end of the third lecture, against the ugliness that dominates so much of contemporary speech and writing.

He was indeed an embodiment of humane letters and thus more than fulfilled the intention in which the Lamar Lectures were established nearly three decades ago by Mrs. Dorothy Blount Lamar: "to provide lectures of the very highest type of scholarship which will aid in the permanent preservation of southern culture, history, and literature." The Lamar Lectures Committee is very glad that the Lectures have been augmented and graced by Cleanth Brooks.

> Michael Cass
> for the
> Lamar Memorial Lectures Committee

THE LANGUAGE
OF THE AMERICAN SOUTH

ONE

Where It Came From

A people (like the English-speaking Irish) which has lost its language may preserve enough of the structure, idiom, intonation and rhythm . . . (vocabulary is of minor importance) for its speech and writing to have qualities not found elsewhere in the language of its adoption.

—T. S. Eliot, *Notes Towards the Definition of Culture*

THOUGH THE COMMITTEE THAT SUPERVISES THE LAMAR Lectures does not insist upon continuity among its lecturers, I suppose that there is something to be said for continuity as a virtue and a convenience.

Professor Richard N. Current's *Northernizing the South,* the twenty-sixth in the Lamar Lectures series, provides me with an obvious point of connection. In his first lecture he relates an amusing anecdote having to do with his first discovery that he too spoke English with an accent. A Southern woman in a country store shocked him by observing, "You know, I've got a cousin in Chicago talks exactly like you." Current goes on to remark: "After that I came to believe and I still believe, that, of all the real or imagined differences between Northerners and Southerners, the speech difference is not only the most noticeable but also the most fundamental."[1]

I agree with him that this speech difference is the most noticeable difference between the Southerner and the citizens from the rest of the country. There are many of his other observations to which I can give only partial assent or, in some instances, none at all. But here he has hit the nail solidly on the head. I must add, however, that I attach far more significance to this speech difference than he apparently does. For in calling it the most "noticeable but also the most fundamental" difference between the North and the South, he implies that the speech difference is really not very important. That is, he seems to be saying that if the most fundamental difference between the Northerner and the Southerner is the way in which they speak the English language, then they are really very much alike.

I have to disagree. The soul of a people is embodied in the language peculiar to them. Look at the way in which the Welsh still jealously cling to their own language even though for centuries Wales has been tied to England by the most powerful of political and economic connections. Consider the importance that the people of Quebec attach to their provincial French—not only in their everyday speech but even in their street signs, shop signs, and formal documents. Remember that a country as tiny as Belgium maintains two languages, French and Flemish.

The cases that I cite are, I grant, special and extreme. The difference between the language of the South and the English spoken in this country at large is not a difference of such magnitude. But more extreme cases may fairly be used to establish a point.

It is significant that peoples throughout history have often stubbornly held on to their native language or dialect because they regarded it as a badge of their identity and because they felt that only through it could they express their inner beings, their attitudes and emotions, and even their own concepts of reality.

Listen to James Joyce's Stephen Dedalus in *A Portrait of the Artist as a Young Man:* "The language in which we [Stephen and the dean of studies, an Englishman] are speaking is his before it is mine. How different are the words *home, Christ, ale, master* on his lips and on mine! I cannot speak or write these words without unrest of spirit. His language, so familiar and so foreign, will always be for me an acquired speech. I have not made or accepted its words. My voice holds them at bay. My soul frets in the shadow of his language."[2]

That the South has its own idiom is tacitly conceded, I believe, by nearly everybody. Outsiders acknowledge that this is so by their amusement at what appears to them a very quaint English, or more emphatically by occasionally having to declare that they simply can't make out what is being said. But the most solid testimony to the individual quality is to be found in its literature and particularly in that rich outpouring of verse and prose during our own century.

Though I give proper credit to the individual literary talent manifested by those who have created this literature, I mean in these lectures to pay special tribute to the language itself—a language that they have inherited and which they have managed to use so well. It has proved to be a valuable and indeed indispensable resource.

Where did this language, or (if I must speak more cautiously) this idiom and dialect, come from? Is it a corruption of proper English? A discoloring of the clear waters issuing from the well of English pure and undefiled? An examination of the case will clearly reveal that no distortion or perversion has occurred, and indeed far less innovation has occurred than one might have supposed. The Southern dialect has perfectly sound historical roots.

I must warn you, however, that in what I shall be saying on this subject I cannot claim to be speaking as an expert. From the beginning, my basic training has been in literature. I am not by profession a language scholar. I am rather, in this field, an amateur, though an enthusiastic amateur. I am still trying to find out where the Southern dialect really came from.

Let me begin by making a few remarks about American pronunciation generally. In spite of our borrowings of words from other languages, French, Spanish, and German, for example, and in spite of our coinage of new words such as *OK, kodak,* and *razz-matazz,* American English obviously derives from the English that was spoken in Great Britain several centuries ago. As far as pronunciation is concerned, we Americans speak an old-fashioned English. Contrary to what the layman assumes, in pronunciation it is the mother language that usually changes, not the daughter language. Let me illustrate.

The so-called broad *a* which in London or Oxford English is used in such words as *last, path, laugh,* and which the Englishman pronounces [la:st], [pa:θ], [la:f], the *ah* vowel was in the motherland a relatively late newcomer. It probably was not adopted into Standard English until some time in the nineteenth century,[3] whereas the settlement of North America by Englishmen occurred in the seventeenth century. Naturally, these Americans-to-be brought across the Atlantic the pronunciation they used at home. After all, it was the only one they knew.

Let's take another example, the so-called dropping of the -*g* in such words as *going, doing, thinking.* Apparently as late as the nineteenth century everyone in England, including the educated classes, dropped his -*g*'s in such words.[4] I used to startle my graduate students at Yale by pointing out that, on the evidence of their rhymes, Wordsworth, Coleridge, Byron, Shelley, and Keats, those glories of English literature of the early nineteenth century, apparently dropped their -*g*'s regularly. Small wonder, then, that most Americans also dropped theirs, and, as your own ears will inform you, here in the South many still do, for the South remains the most conservative part of the United States. My guess is that the restoration of the -*g* was a spelling pronunciation, the result of the Victorian schoolmarm and her American counterpart, who insisted that these words must be pronounced just as they were spelled: don't let a perfectly good -*g* go to waste.

As I have already remarked, we Americans in our pronunciation are in general old-fashioned,[5] those of us here in the South probably the most old-fashioned of all. The coastal regions of the South apparently got their characteristic pronunciations early and are, along with the Southern regions that have been heavily influenced by them, loath to give them up.

Does the pronunciation of the coastal South differ from that of the other regions of the United States simply because it has retained its old-fashioned pronunciations, whereas the other regions have adopted new ones? An even more interesting question is this: Why are there marked differences between the Southern pronunciation and that of regions which were also very early settled, such as the eastern coast of Massachusetts?

These two early settled regions do agree, contrary to the rest of the country, in dropping the consonant *r* when it occurs finally, or before another consonant. Thus, the Southerner pronounces *never* as *nev-uh* and *barn* as *bahn*. The man from Massachusetts Bay agrees in dropping the *r*, but he pronounces *barn* as ba:n. His *a* is a vowel between the vowel of *cat* and that of *ah*. So there would seem to be another factor at work in accounting for some of these dialectal differences. It has to do with place as well as time—specifically, with the part of England from which the early colonists of each region originally came.

The belief that place of origin is important is further reinforced by the fact that in their treatment of the consonant *r*, those early settled regions of our country, both North and South, in this matter differ from the rest of the United States but do approximate the pronunciation of present-day standard British English. The general old-fashioned character of the American English will scarcely account for this phenomenon.

My particular concern on this occasion is, of course, with Coastal or Lowland Southern, and such research as I have done is pretty much limited to this dialect, though I may observe that some features of the eastern New Englander's dialect, such as his *a* where we here use *ah*, do seem to point to East Anglia, that is, to English counties like Norfolk, Suffolk, and Essex.[6]

In speaking of the Southern Lowland dialect, let me begin by referring to an article on the pronunciation of a particular city in this area, that of Charleston, South Carolina. The author, Raven I. McDavid, than whom there was no greater authority on this matter of the American dialects, writes that the earliest settlers of Charleston "appear to have been predominantly from Southern England."[7] But can we narrow down the southern counties of England in question, and does this influence of the English southern counties apply to other variations of the dialect of the American South? Yet even if such a determination should prove to be possible, you will, of course, hardly expect me to demonstrate it in the brief time allowed for this lecture.

Even so, I hope to be able to set forth some interesting resemblances between some of the county dialects of southern England and the dialect which most of us will recognize to be the typical dialect of the lowland or plantation South. Note that I am not including in this statement the Southern hill or mountain dialect, which the specialists prefer to call Southern Midland. Though in many ways it resembles Coastal Southern, it shows significant differences.

The resemblances between Coastal Southern and the dialect of the southern counties of England can be put most strikingly by using the "broadest" Southern dialect that I can think of, namely, that of Joel Chandler Harris's famous Uncle Remus. The choice of his dialect has an additional advantage: it is probably thoroughly familiar to most of my audience.

Would you expect to learn that when Uncle Remus has Brer Rabbit remark that he is "gwine" to town, he is using a word that Thomas Hardy, at about the same time, was putting in the mouths of the Dorsetshire countrymen who figure in his famous Wessex novels? Dorset is a southwestern county of England.[8]

When Uncle Remus pronounces *mercy* as *massy* (as in the expression "Law's a-massy") he uses a pronunciation that was still to be heard in several of the southern counties of England as late as the twentieth century. If he pronounces *pert* as *peart*, so do (or did until recently) the country folk of the south of England and also of other counties farther north.[9] Some of you in the audience have heard, I am sure, *peart* from the lips of elderly white people in our own Southern states. I heard it in my boyhood in west Tennessee.

Allow me to offer one more of these phonetic resemblances. When I first noticed Uncle Remus's pronunciation of *muskmelon*, which Joel Chandler Harris sets down as *mush-*

million, I assumed that if Harris had really heard it correctly
this pronunciation (or mispronunciation) must have arisen
from the black man's inability to cope with the English language. Nevertheless, I looked up *muskmelon* in the *Oxford English Dictionary,* and to my astonishment found that it did
record the form *mushmillion* and, wonder of wonders, re-
ported that it was so spelled in a letter written in 1592 by a
Dorsetshire man. Dorset, I remind you, is one of the southwestern counties of England.

Unless you are willing to believe that in finding instances
like these we are stumbling on mere coincidences, then
some sort of relationship must have existed between the dialects of England's southern counties and our popular
Southern pronunciation even in its "broadest" forms.

Some years ago I bought from a British bookseller a little
paperback pamphlet which purported to give the King
James version of *The Song of Solomon* as it would have been
spoken by a countryman or villager of Sussex.[10] Sussex is a
county about forty or fifty miles south of London. Here is
the way the Sussex version begins:

De song of songs, dat is Solomon's,
Let him kiss me wud de kisses of his mouth; for yer love is
better dan wine.
Cause of de smell of yer good intments, yer naüm is lik intment
tipped out; derefore de maidens love ye. . . .
Look not upan me, cause I be black, cause de sun has shoun
upan me; my mother's childun was mad wud me; dey maüd me
kipper of de vineyards; but my own vineyard I han't kipt.

And the Sussex version goes on in this vein through the
entire eight chapters. Here are three more characteristic
verses:

My beloved spoke, an said to me: Git up, my love, my fair un, an come away. [2:10]

Jest a liddle while âhter I passed by em, I foun him dat my soul loves. . . . [3:4]

I charge ye, O ye dahters of Jerusalem, by de roes and by de hinds of de fil, dat you doänt rouse up nor wake my love, tull such-time as he likes. [3:5]

Now this pamphlet was not printed until 1860, and I can assure you that the villagers and the countrymen of this essentially rural county had probably never seen a black man, let alone heard one speak, in their entire lives. If the resemblances between the Sussex dialect of 1860 and the Negro dialects of the Southern states just before the Civil War do amount to something more than pure happenstance, then what is the nature of the relation? Clearly the men of Sussex did not derive their dialect from the American blacks. Did the black people of our Southern states then derive their dialect from the dialects of such English counties as Sussex? If so, what was the link?

The only link I can conceive of is this: the Englishmen who emigrated to the Southern states and from whom the black man necessarily had to learn his English—from whom else could he have learned it?—must have come predominantly from the counties of southern England.[11]

Yet the proof, even if I had it fully in hand, cannot be presented succinctly—certainly not in the course of this lecture. What I propose to do, therefore, is to take up only one of the most striking features common to the dialect of earlier Sussex and that of Uncle Remus, and see what grounds there may be for taking the resemblances seriously as evidence of a causal relation. The pronunciation of *the, this,* and *that,* as *de, dis,* and *dat* is the feature I have in mind.

In a sense, mine will amount to an *a fortiori* argument. One deliberately chooses a case that is the most difficult to establish; but if one can establish it, all the easier cases fall into place as proved or probable. Most of you here, I dare say, will take my theory about *de, dis,* and *dat* to involve such an argument. For to many, it will seem incredible that the Negro derived this pronunciation originally from the whites, for did Southern white men ever say *de, dis,* and *dat?*

There are several other reasons for choosing to treat in detail this particular feature of the Uncle Remus dialect. One thing that one needs to know is what the English county dialects were like back in the seventeenth century, when emigration to the American colonies was going on. Although the scholars of an earlier day were not much interested in giving an exact account of them, yet a feature as special as this one had a good chance of coming to notice early, and this one did. William Bullokar, himself a Sussex man, mentions it as a pronunciation used in east Sussex and Kent. Bullokar was born in about 1530.[12] So we have every reason to believe that *de, dis,* and *dat* were being used in Sussex as early as the Tudor age. Thus, any of the common folk of east Sussex and the neighboring county of Kent who set out for Virginia or the Carolinas might have brought with them such a pronunciation.

If someone of you wonders whether there were not noblemen from this part of England who, of course, must have spoken the standard language and no dialect at all, I must tell you that the facts are heavily against any such supposition. At this time the standard language had hardly settled down to a generally acknowledged form. Sir Walter Raleigh, we are told, even at Elizabeth's court spoke broad Devonshire to his dying day.[13] Besides, the younger sons of English peers were few enough in the new American colonies. We did receive, to be sure, as the sequel showed, plenty of sound stock from old England, but it is notorious that those who emigrate to the colonies usually do so to better their fortunes. If they already enjoy good estate at home, why leave it? There were doubtless occasional exceptions, but not many, we may be sure.

So *de, dis,* and *dat* go at least as far back as the early sixteenth century. Moreover, these forms are attested not merely in the little book of 1860 from which I have quoted, but by other authorities: W. P. Parish in 1887, Alexander J. Ellis in 1889, and Joseph Wright in 1905.[14] Since these authorities indicated that the *d*-forms were already extinct in Kent and almost so in Sussex, I took for granted that they had totally died out by the beginning of our century. But Raven McDavid, who kindly looked over this material shortly before his death, suggested that, in order to be sure, I should consult the latest survey of the English dialects. I did so and found that in the 1960s *d*-forms still survived, though barely, in Kent as well as in Sussex.[15]

So much for the English side. What about America? In particular, is there any evidence that white men living in the Southern states ever used these pronunciations? There is. In a study of the dialect of east Alabama published early in this century, L. W. Payne records that some of them did, especially elderly people living in rural neighborhoods.[16] Payne, naturally in his day, interpreted that fact as a borrowing by the whites from the blacks. But the fact that the borrowers were elderly and living out in the country far from centers of population and often without much schooling points to the reverse circumstance: the dying out of an earlier form.

In any case, Sumner Ives, in a study published in 1954, records that *de, dis,* and *dat* were still to be heard in the

South from the lips of elderly people, including elderly white people.[17] His information comes from the field records of *The Linguistic Atlas of the United States*. In a recent letter to me, Raven McDavid, an editor of *The Linguistic Atlas*, tells me that he knows of two educated white Southerners who still use *de, dis,* and *dat*.

Why, then, have such forms persisted among the blacks while almost completely vanishing among the whites? The answer should be obvious. The blacks, who were at first denied education and later on got only a rather poor and limited "book learning," held on to what their ancestors had learned by ear and which had been passed on to them through oral tradition. In short, they rather faithfully preserved what they had heard, were little influenced by spelling, and in general actually served as a conservative force.

To say this is not at all to deny that the blacks influenced the language—through their intonation, through their own rhythms, through the development of striking metaphors, new word coinages, and fresh idioms. It should, however, free them from the charge that they corrupted and perverted the pronunciation of "pure English."

At the risk of allowing this topic to become tedious, I think I must call your attention to one further bit of evidence, for I count it of great importance. A common explanation of the black man's pronunciation (or mispronunciation) of words like *the, this,* and *that* is that he was unable to pronounce the so-called *th* sound, just as for a Frenchman, a German, or an Italian this consonant is completely unfamiliar and hard to form properly.

Such an explanation may in fact account for such failures in Gullah, the dialect spoken by the black people on the Sea Islands of South Carolina and Georgia. I know too little about that special dialect to speak about it in an informed manner, and I except it as a special case from the present discussion. The Gullahs were relatively isolated and had little contact with the whites, and their dialect may well have been influenced by their native African languages.

Uncle Remus apparently has no trouble with the voiceless *th:* he can say *thin, think,* and *thank* perfectly well. It is the voiced *th* that he regularly converts to a *d,* and this is exactly the distinction that the yeomen of Sussex and Kent were making back in the seventeenth century and continued to make for two centuries later.

Uncle Remus's friend Daddy Jack is said to be a Gullah, and so he says "I t'ink so" as well as "Dat is so." But you will not find Uncle Remus, though ever a courteous man, saying "T'ank 'ee." If we are hoping to find the roots of Uncle Remus's speech, his preservation of that distinction may prove an important clue.[18]

I said earlier that I was putting forward a hypothesis, not a proved or perhaps even probable conclusion. But even a hypothesis deserves fair treatment. Allow me then to restate mine with a few reservations.

The language of the South almost certainly came from the south of England. I have emphasized the southeastern corner, Kent and Sussex. But it would be stupid to claim that those who first came to our Southern coasts came exclusively from those counties.[19] Obviously, they came from many others as well. The eastern county of Essex, the northern neighbor of Kent, may well have influenced our dialect also. Lastly, the seventeenth-century speech of London itself was probably quite important. Lest you bristle at the suggestion that we Southerners speak an earlier version of Cockney, let me remind you that the early speech of London was also the direct ancestor of the standard British English of today. If the English of the court, of the ancient universities, and of the church came, as time passed, to deviate from the Cockney of Dickens's nineteenth-century novels and from Bernard Shaw's twentieth-century *Pygmalion*, our Southern speech, you may be sure, also came to differ from it too; very greatly, I would say, and perhaps not by changing from its seventeenth-century form so much as by simply standing still. Like Standard English, Cockney went on to develop into its present form. Anyway, we mustn't be snobbish. We ought to be able to admit that the speech of Shaw's Eliza Doolittle may possibly be a third cousin once removed of our own.

Of course pronunciation is only one aspect of a language. Its vocabulary, its characteristic figurative expressions and sayings, its idioms and locutions, its rhythms and "speech tune" are very important. They are particularly important to the writer of fiction, poetry, or plays. So it is with features of this sort that I shall be principally concerned in my next two lectures as I discuss the richness of the Southern language as a resource for its writers.

Yet can such features also be traced back to old England? With far less certainty, I should say. But even so, there are lots of intriguing hints. For example, in my childhood in west Tennessee, one could say that the itch of a chiggerbite "terrified" him, though the speaker certainly did not mean to say that he was suffering excruciating fear or mortal terror. If you look into the *Oxford English Dictionary* you will find that in the standard language *terrify* once had as one of its meanings "to irritate or torment." John Milton himself used it in this sense. Though this meaning is now obsolete in Standard English, it is still to be found in the country dialects all over England, just as it is still to be found in our Southern states.

One can even find in the country dialects of the southeastern corner of England hints of the celebrated "Southern drawl." Thus W. P. Parish observes that the Sussex dialect is "rather drawling" in effect[20] and the editor of the Sussex *Song of Solomon,* from which I quoted earlier, tells us in his preliminary notes that in the dialect of Sussex "the vowel 'a' is very broadly pronounced as if it were followed by 'u'; thus 'taste' is best expressed as taüst," and so he spells it t-a-u-s-t, but he carefully places a dieresis over the *u* so that the reader will not mistakenly take the pronunciation to be *tawst* but will understand that the *u* merely indicates a lengthened glide. If I am interpreting him correctly, the pronunciation would be one that you might well hear on the streets of Macon today. The editor treats the long *o* of *goat* or *boat* in the same way.

But enough of these speculations about the possible origins of our Southern language. If my hypotheses are to be made good, the task will demand a whole book of further exploration and the accumulation of pertinent evidence. I hardly need to say that this book remains to be written. My next two lectures will be devoted to some of the ways in which our writers have put this language to effective use.

TWO

The Language of the Gentry and the Folk

For the transmission of a culture—a peculiar way of thinking, feeling and behaving—and for its maintenance, there is no safeguard more reliable than a language.

—T. S. Eliot, *Notes Towards the Definition of Culture*

IN MY FIRST LECTURE I WAS PRINCIPALLY CONCERNED WITH the origins of our Southern language, and I offered a provisional account of where it originated. In my next two lectures I shall be primarily concerned with that language as a literary resource, providing examples from Southern writers, past and present, to show how they have used it.

These examples will fall into two main categories: the colloquial language, the speech of the folk, including the more illiterate dialects, both black and white; and the more formal speech and writing of the gentry and the professional classes.

It is, of course, easier to illustrate the more striking "Southern" peculiarities from the colloquial and dialectal forms of the language, for these obviously deviate farthest from present-day Standard English, whatever one takes that standard to be. Yet I believe that I can show that even in the more formal language of the South there is a distinctly Southern quality. Moreover, I shall, in the course of these lectures, be arguing that the strength of even the more formal Southern writers stems from their knowledge of and rapport with the language spoken by the unlettered. Most of our writers have in fact recognized the colloquial and even dialectal aspects for what they are: dialects of great vitality and power, dialects capable of eloquence and even of a kind of folk poetry. Our best writers have never held in contempt the speech of the folk or used it only for comic effects. Such matters as these I now hope to explore more fully and illustrate concretely.

Let me begin this second lecture, however, by showing how one of our foremost Southern men of letters stated the relationship among the various strata of a language which he knew so well. He is Allen Tate, and many of you here present must have read his novel *The Fathers*. It has sometimes been called the finest "first novel" ever written. I believe that this praise is entirely just, and *The Fathers* was also the last and only novel that he ever wrote: at once an arrival and a departure in glory.

You will remember that in this novel Lacy Buchan, born about 1845, relates the story of what happened to his family during the Civil War and in the postwar years. Early in the story he has this to say about his own father:

I may as well say here that my father did not speak dialect but the standard English of the eighteenth century. In pronunciation the criterion was the oral tradition, not the way the word looked in print to an uneducated school-teacher. For example, although he wrote *ate*, he pronounced it *et*, as if it were the old past tense, *eat*. He used the double negative in conversation, as well as *ain't*, and he spoke the language with great ease at four levels: first, the level just described, conversation among family and friends; second, the speech of the "plain people" abounding in many archaisms; third, the speech of the Negroes, which was merely late

seventeenth or early eighteenth-century English ossified; and,
fourth, the Johnsonian diction appropriate to formal occasions, a
style that he could wield in perfect sentences four hundred words
long. He would not have understood our conception of "correct
English." Speech was like manners, an expression of sensibility
and taste.[1]

This seems to me an excellent account of the state of af-
fairs just prior to the War Between the States, though I
would want to make a few adjustments and refinements.
But I have no serious quarrel with Allen Tate's very percep-
tive account. It represents a giant's step beyond the received
opinion of 1938 when *The Fathers* first appeared and, I make
bold to say, beyond even that commonly held today.

In 1835, ten years before Lacy Buchan is supposed to
have been born, Augustus Baldwin Longstreet published
his famous *Georgia Scenes*. As one would expect of a lawyer,
clergyman, and college president-to-be, Longstreet wrote a
rather elegant prose style. It reminded Poe of Joseph Addison's *Spectator Papers* rather than the style of Dr. Samuel
Johnson. But in any case, it was excellent eighteenth-century prose. Nevertheless, the subject matter of *Georgia Scenes*
was the goings-on of the plain people at their dances, fist-
fights, horse races, and gander-pullings. Longstreet did not
make the mistake of filling the mouths of those rough-hewn
folk with Addisonian prose. He lets them use their native
Doric. Indeed, much of Longstreet's humor consists in the
contrast between the Addisonian prose in which, as an observer, he reports their antics and the quite earthy idiom
employed by these same characters when they speak. Thus,
in "The Horse-Swap" the narrator described an uncommonly unprepossessing nag, Bullet by name, with elegant
though gingerly irony. Longstreet as observer writes:

Nature had done but little for Bullet's head and neck; but he managed, in a great measure, to hide their defects by bowing perpetually. He had obviously suffered severely for corn; but if his ribs and hip bones had not disclosed the fact, *he* never would have done it; for he was in all respects as cheerful and happy as if he commanded all the corn-cribs and fodder-stacks in Georgia.[2]

But the two braggart horsetraders are allowed to speak for themselves in their own way. After a great deal of jockeying for position and making offer and counteroffer, the one who calls himself Blossom swears that he

"never would be backed out for three dollars after bantering a man"; and accordingly, [the two] closed the trade.

"Now," said Blossom, as he handed Peter the three dollars, "I'm a man that, when he makes a bad trade, makes the most of it until he can make a better. I'm for no rues and after-claps."

"That's just my way," said Peter; "I never goes to law to mend my bargains."[3]

I must admit that at a first reading their jargon quite put me off. How do you "banter" a man? And what are "rues" and "after-claps"? *Rues* turned out to be rather easy; it means "regrets," though in our day it has become something of a poetic word. Remembering Housman's "With rue my heart is laden / For golden friends I had," one hardly expects to hear it uttered matter-of-factly by these rowdies of the Georgia backwoods. *After-claps* turns out to be of quite ancient lineage. The first occurrence recorded by the *Oxford English Dictionary* is in the early fifteenth century. It means "an unsuspected stroke [delivered in a contest] after the recipient has ceased to be on his guard"—a surprise blow suddenly delivered after the fight is thought to be over.

The meaning of *banter* is far more complicated. It can mean to chaff or ridicule, and both of Longstreet's horse-traders have indeed been ridiculing each other's prowess as traders as well as the sorry nags that each is trying to put off on the other. But *banter* can also mean "to do someone out of something by ridicule," and it can mean "to challenge one's opponent to a match or a race"; and something of this last meaning seems present here too.

Apparently *banter* began in the seventeenth century as a slang term. Jonathan Swift deplored it early in the eighteenth century as too undignified to deserve admission into the language. So the difference between Blossom's term and Longstreet's more elegant language is not that his illiterate Georgian's word is a coinage of the American frontier, but that, though it originated on the other side of the Atlantic, it was from the beginning a word of low repute—not from Addison's elegant pages, but from the shadier purlieus of the London underworld.

Longstreet's way of playing off the language of the illiterate against the language of the educated is only one of the many ways in which the language of the folk can be used for literary effect.

Consider the characteristic method used by Joel Chandler Harris. Harris employs the dialect as it issues from the lips of Uncle Remus without ironic intent. He clearly admires its power to express the old man's wit and wisdom. I find absolutely no condescension—no disparagement of it as a proper medium for literary expression. Quite the contrary. He seems to treat his favorite narrator with affectionate respect. But Harris clearly saw and explicitly declared that to tell the animal stories without the dialect was to divest them of most of their charm.

Uncle Remus is allowed to win every encounter with his employer, Miss Sally. He remains in thorough control of every situation. Moreover, his stories abound in sound insights into the human situation. Their comedy is firmly grounded in reality. His Brer Rabbit is not the cute Easter bunny. He is devious; he can even be cruel. Yet finally, for all his prowess, he is not made to appear invulnerable. Uncle Remus sometimes represents him as defeated, as if he occasionally became too clever for his own good. That, I should say, is his ultimate compliment to his favorite character. Brer Rabbit is no demigod, no pre-Disneyan super-rabbit.

Though in my first lecture I used the Uncle Remus tales principally to enforce parallels with the English county dialects, I do not mean to pay less than homage to their quality as literature. One of my special favorites is "Brother Rabbit Has Fun at the Ferry" (1892). The ferry in question is a flat boat, a kind of raft, pulled by hand across the stream. The ferryman is Brer B'ar, a physical type, justly proud of his muscles but not very powerful in matters of the intellect, and so he admires feats of the mind that are quite beyond him.

A horseman asks to be conveyed across the stream, but his horse refuses to step onto the ferryboat. Brer Rabbit sits on a stump as an amused observer, enjoying what he later insists were simply the highjinks of some fun-loving creatures.

In any case, the mare defeats every device of her rider and of Brer B'ar to get her onto the ferry. Finally Brer B'ar asks for Brer Rabbit's help, and Brer Rabbit consents to help, though he continues to maintain that he had taken the whole business to have been play-acting. He says:

"What de name er goodness is you all tryin' ter do down dar? What kinder capers is you cuttin' up? I bin settin' here watchin' you, des dyin' er laughin' at de way you and de man en dem creeturs been gwine on."[4]

He quickly allows himself, however, to be persuaded that the problem is real, and suggests that the mare's colt be put on the raft first; and sure enough, its mother quickly takes her place beside it. Brer B'ar tells his customer "what er soon creetur Brer Rabbit is, dat nobody can't fool 'im en nobody can't outdo him."[5]

Mr. Man is so much impressed that on his return he sets another problem to test Brer Rabbit's sagacity, and again Brer Rabbit easily solves the problem. But Mr. Man won't give up. He wagers a pot of honey that Brer Rabbit can't answer his next question. He holds over his head a little basket and defies the rabbit to tell him what is in it.

Brer Rabbit study, en den he 'low, sezee, "*De sparrer* [that is, the sparrow] *kin tell you.*"

De man look at 'im hard, en den he say, sezee, "What kinder creetur is you, nohow?"[6]

Sure enough, the basket contains a bird's nest with a sparrow in it, and Mr. Man gives Brer Rabbit the honey pot. His parting remark is, "You er one er deze yer graveyard rabbits, dat what you is"—to which the Rabbit's reply is simply laughter.

The little boy to whom Uncle Remus is telling the story naturally wants to know how Brer Rabbit knew about the sparrow—as do, I suppose, all the rest of us. But Uncle Remus immediately corrects him:

"Who say he know it, honey?"

"Didn't you say so?"

"Shoo, honey, freshun up yo' 'membunce. When de man ax Brer Rabbit What in dat? he make answer dat a sparrer kin tell 'im kaze a sparrer flyin' roun' kin see what in de basket."

"Well," said the little boy, with a sigh, "I thought Brother Rabbit knew."

"Luck tol' 'im, honey; Brer Rabbit wuz a mighty man fer luck."[7]

And so the story ends, in my opinion, neatly and with sufficient point. Brer Rabbit is the slight little fellow who lives by his wits, and possesses enough wits to keep himself alive. But for the most part, he is able to avoid the sin of *hubris*. Besides, since Mr. Man had put to him an impossible and therefore unfair test, he was quite right to give a riddling answer; and if Tyche, the goddess of luck, arranged for it to pay off with a double bonus, why should the wise man or rabbit scorn such help?

I have remarked earlier that dialect speech and the speech of more or less illiterate characters will usually yield more obvious examples of distinctive "Southern" linguistic traits. The reason is clear. The literate writer is drawing upon the whole of the English literary tradition. He has read his Shakespeare and his Milton, his Wordsworth and his Dickens. But to concede this is not at all to say that a regional quality is not sufficiently manifest even in such writing, though to discern it will require a more delicate sense of style.

For a start, one might consider the following passages in Allen Tate's *The Fathers*. Lacy Buchan is now sixteen years old; it is the first year of the Civil War. A catastrophe has occurred. George Posey, Lacy's brother-in-law, after provocation but on impulse, shoots and kills Lacy's elder brother. After this harrowing experience Lacy has started on foot for his home in northern Virginia. Confused, distraught, and light of head with a fever, he imagines that his grandfather, a Virgini͟ ͞f the old school, is now walking beside him and with grandfau͟͟͞ ͥͭ͜ is trying to explain George Posey's action.

We went out of the gate, carefully replacing the bars, and went up the road a hundred yards and sat down on a pile of fence rails by the roadside to rest again and to think it over again as best we could. He didn't mean to do it, I said to my grandfather, and he said: No, it was not the intention of your brother-in-law to kill your brother. It is never, my son, his intention to do any evil but he does evil because he has not the will to do good. The only expectancy that he shares with humanity is the pursuing grave, and the thought of extinction overwhelms him because he is entirely alone. My son, in my day we were never alone, as your brother-in-law is alone. He is alone like a tornado. His one purpose is to whirl and he brushes aside the obstacles in his way. My son, you are a classical scholar and you have read the epic of Apollonius of Rhodes, the Alexandrian scholar who pieced together from many older authors the pathetic tale of Jason and Medea and the Golden Fleece. Jason was a handsome young blade of royal descent who had suffered much from a violent family in his youth, so that nothing ordinary interested him; and he called together a great party of heroes and went off after the wool of a remarkable ram [the ram that bore the golden fleece].[8]

In his description of George Posey, the phantom grandfather paints a striking portrait of the alienated man of our own time. But in the grandfather's account you can hear the cadences of the eighteenth century—as, of course, Allen Tate meant for his reader to hear them.

Or, for another example, listen to the following passage from Robert Penn Warren's *All the King's Men.* As most of you know, the story has to do with a well-known Southern politician of fifty years ago, but in order to point up the alienation and confusion of his twentieth-century hero, Jack Burden, Warren needs a historical backdrop for contrast. He provides it in Cass Mastern's account of his own brief life. Cass died comparatively young of wounds incurred in the Civil War. But he had deliberately sought his death, for he was tormented with guilt and anguish at having betrayed his best friend. He had seduced (or more accurately, allowed himself to be seduced by) that friend's wife. In the passage I shall read Cass describes the occasion of his betrayal.

When she first entered the room, in which the shades of approaching twilight were gathering though the hour for the candles to be lit had scarcely come, I thought that her eyes were black, and the effect was most striking, her hair being of such a fairness. I noticed, too, how softly she trod and with a gliding motion which, though she was perhaps of a little less than moderate stature, gave an impression of regal dignity—

and Cass quotes the Latin of the passage in the *Aeneid* which describes the appearance of Venus to Aeneas, ending with the words

Et vera incessu patuit Dea.

So the Mantuan said, when Venus appeared and the true goddess was revealed by her gait. She came into the room and was the true goddess as revealed in her movement, and was, but for Divine Grace (if such be granted to a parcel of corruption such as I), my true damnation. She gave me her hand and spoke with a tingling huskiness which made me think of rubbing my hand upon a soft deep-piled cloth, like velvet, or upon a fur. It would not have been called a musical voice such as is generally admired. I know that, but I can only set down what effect it worked upon my own organs of hearing.[9]

To my ear this is a beautiful reenactment of the prose of the antebellum South, with its careful grammar, its stately cadences, and its classical allusions and quotations.

For those of you who feel that I am fudging a bit in my eagerness to represent distinctively Southern prose as spoken by the educated, you might compare from this same novel Warren's representation of the speech of Judge Irwin, a gentleman of the old school, though living in the 1930s. He does not speak like Cass Mastern, but then neither does he speak like a character out of a novel by Henry James or Edith Wharton, or, to come down to the 1930s, like a character from a story by Ernest Hemingway.

Full contrast with Cass Mastern and Judge Irwin comes with the speech of another character from Warren's novel, Governor Willie Stark, the Southern populist politician. Stark is equally impressive in his bitterly contemptuous treatment of his underlings and in his flights of oratory. Observing Willie Stark in full eruption is like observing an active and apparently inexhaustible volcano. Here is Willie on the hustings:

"Folks, there's going to be a leetle mite of trouble back in town. Between me and that Legislature-ful of hyena-headed, feist-faced, belly-dragging sons of slack-gutted she-wolves. If you know what I mean. Well, I been looking at them and their kind so long, I just figured I'd take me a little trip and see what human folks looked like in the face before I clean forgot. Well, you all look human. More or less. And sensible. In spite of what they're saying back in that Legislature and getting paid five dollars a day of your tax money for saying it. They're saying you didn't have bat sense or goose gumption when you cast your sacred ballot to elect me Governor of this state.[10]

There are no classical allusions or stately cadences here. But his speech is, nevertheless, intensely Southern. It's not the way Mayor Koch of New York City or Walter Mondale or Ronald Reagan harangues the crowd.

Warren also has a full mastery of the speech of the Southern mountains and hill country. An excellent example is provided by the dialect of a character named Ashby Wyndham in *At Heaven's Gate* (1941). Though Ashby's speech varies markedly from Coastal Southern, there is between the two varieties a large overlap of common elements. Like the Coastal dialect, the Hill Southern represents an old fashioned English in its vocabulary and syntax. Here follows a sample from the "statement" that Ashby makes about his life.

[Marie] would be done work and I would be waitin. Ax or layin to a crosscut all day, and I would see her comin out of that there kitchen and me waitin in the dark and the weariness was not nuthin. It was lak I was wakin up fresh and a sunbeam done smote you on the eyeball and roused you. We would go to them frolics at Massey on Saturday night. She would stand quiet and watch them folks dance and stomp and the caller called the figgers and them fiddles goin. She stood right quiet, but you could see the sparkle in her. If you looked clost. Then maybe we would dance a set or twain. But I did not git no more of Barkus moonshine, nor offen nobody else. At least not when I was with Marie. She did not lak for me to. And when I was with Marie I never felt no call.

I never taken to likker lak I use to, and likker is a sin. But a man cannot be good out of plain humankindness. He cannot be good for it ain't in a pore man. He cannot be good unlest it is good in the light of Gods eye. Gods eye ain't on him and he just swaps one sin for another one, and it was worse maybe. I laid off likker but I swapped for another sin. I laid off likker for Marie but it was because of pore human love and not for Gods love.[11]

Discourse of this sort is not comic in its effect, but is serious and creates its own kind of eloquence.

Another of the obvious masters of the various aspects of
the Southern speech is William Faulkner. His range extends
across the whole spectrum of Coastal or Lowland Southern,
literate and illiterate. He gives us the black man speaking
under both comic and tragic circumstances; the speech of
the landed gentry, that of his Sartorises and Compsons,
both men and women; that of the landless white man speaking out of his orneriness and general cussedness; or the yeo-
man white, whether possessed of a few acres or of more,
expressing his homespun decency and integrity. Nor ought
I fail to mention Faulkner's representatives of the newer
generations, young men and women of the late 1920s, '30s,
and '40s, who already have begun to show the stresses and
strains of the new day in the South. They react to the situation each in his own way, but reveal in their reaction the
Southern quality of their speech.

Faulkner, in an abundance of riches, has provided us
with examples of all these and more—much more than I
can illustrate within the compass of this lecture. I must con-
fine myself to a very few cases.

In "Pantaloon in Black," which constitutes the third sec-
tion of *Go Down, Moses* and is one of Faulkner's very finest
stories, Rider, a powerful young black man, has, after only a
few months of happiness, suffered the death of his wife.
After the burial his old aunt and his best friend try to per-
suade him not to go back alone to the cabin where the couple had lived their few happy months together. The reason,
they explain, is that her spirit will still "be wawkin." But
Rider insists on returning, and not because he dismisses as
a mere superstition the possibility that Mannie is walking.
We soon find that he hopes that she is, for he yearns to see
her under any circumstance and under any guise.

When he gets to his cabin door, his dog refuses to enter

and begins to howl; for indeed Mannie is there, "standing in the kitchen door, looking at him."

> "Mannie," he said. "Hit's awright. Ah aint afraid." Then he took a step toward her, slow, not even raising his hand yet, and stopped. Then he took another step. But this time as soon as he moved she began to fade. He stopped at once, not breathing again, motionless, willing his eyes to see that she had stopped too. But she had not stopped. She was fading, going. "Wait," he said, talking as sweet as he had ever heard his voice speak to a woman: "Den lemme go wid you, honey." But she was going.[12]

Then Mannie is gone, and Rider tries again to bring her back. He enters the kitchen and goes to the stove.

> He needed no light. He had set the stove up himself and built the shelves for the dishes, from among which he took two plates by feel and from the pot sitting cold on the cold stove he ladled onto the plates the food which his aunt had brought yesterday and of which he had eaten yesterday though now he did not remember when he had eaten it nor what it was, and carried the plates to the scrubbed bare table beneath the single small fading window and drew two chairs up and sat down, waiting again until he knew his voice would be what he wanted it to be. "Come on hyar, now," he said roughly. "Come on hyar and eat yo supper. Ah aint gonter have no—" and ceased, looking down at his plate, breathing the strong, deep pants, his chest arching and collapsing until he stopped it presently and held himself motionless for perhaps a half minute, and raised a spoonful of the cold and glutinous peas to his mouth. The congealed and lifeless mass seemed to bounce on contact with his lips.[13]

This is the story of Orpheus and his lost Eurydice transposed from classical Greece into north Mississippi and made, let me add, utterly convincing. The dialect in which Rider speaks makes its own contribution. Prettify it or formalize it, and the magical reality is lost.

The following passage from *The Hamlet* also shows Faulkner fashioning a kind of poetry out of what would seem to most people completely unpromising material. I have in mind not only what to many will seem a quite unremarkable landscape, but the coarse, not always grammatical talk of a group of men who have gathered this evening on the porch of Will Varner's crossroads general store.

They walked in a close clump, tramping their shadows into the road's mild dust, blotting the shadows of the burgeoning trees which soared, trunk branch and twig against the pale sky, delicate and finely thinned. They passed the dark store. Then the pear tree came in sight. It rose in mazed and silver immobility like exploding snow; the mockingbird still sang in it. "Look at that tree," Varner said. "It ought to make this year, sho."

"Corn'll make this year too," one said.

"A moon like this is good for every growing thing outen earth," Varner said. "I mind when we and Mrs. Varner was expecting Eula. Already had a mess of children and maybe we ought to quit them. But I wanted some more gals. Others had done married and moved away, and a passel of boys, soon as they get big enough to be worth anything, they aint got time to work. Got to set around store and talk. But a gal will stay home and work until she does get married. So there was a old woman told my mammy once that if a woman showed her belly to the full moon after she had done caught, it would be a gal. So Mrs. Varner taken and laid every night with the moon on her nekid belly, until it fulled and after. I could lay my ear to her belly and hear Eula kicking and scrouging like all get-out, feeling the moon."[14]

Some of you may be thinking: Yes, the description of the pear tree is perhaps a kind of poetry, though the image of "exploding snow" may be going too far. But what about earthy old Will Varner's anecdote? Is it a celebration of the powers of fertility, a bit of stupid folk belief, or something close to bawdy? Well, I would suggest that these men, who have little or no book learning, are, almost in spite of themselves, giving testimony to the beauty and power of nature, which makes the earth renew itself every springtime, and of which power the moon has always seemed to primitive man a fit emblem.

My next example also comes from *The Hamlet*. It is from the famous auction of the wild ponies brought from Texas to be sold to Mississippi farmers who do not need them, cannot afford them, and, as it proves, cannot even catch them when they break out of the lot in which they are now penned up. So the scene is a not too thinly veiled satire on modern advertising as well as a display of rhetoric put to the service of cutthroat salesmanship.

The antics of the spotted ponies that the Texan wants to sell truly test his mettle as an auctioneer. As they charge and career around the lot, it is perfectly plain that they are wild, completely unbroken to the saddle or to harness of any kind. More than that, they are utterly vicious. But the Texan is undaunted.

"Them ponies is gentle as a dove, boys. The man that buys them will get the best piece of horseflesh he ever forked or druv for the money. Naturally they got spirit; I aint selling crowbait. Besides, who'd want Texas crowbait anyway, with Mississippi full of it?" His stare was still absent and unwinking; there was no mirth or humor in his voice and there was neither mirth nor humor in the single guffaw which came from the rear of the group. Two wagons were now drawing out of the road at the same time, up to the fence. The men got down from them and tied them to the fence and approached. "Come up, boys," the Texan said. "You're just in time to buy a good gentle horse cheap."15

The Texan makes another attempt to quiet the crowd's worry about buying these equine wildcats.

"Now, boys, . . . Who says that pony aint worth fifteen dollars? You couldn't buy that much dynamite for just fifteen dollars. There aint one of them cant do a mile in three minutes; turn them into pasture and they will board themselves; work them like hell all day and every time you think about it, lay them over the head with a single-tree and after a couple of days every jack rabbit one of them will be so tame you will have to put them out of the house at night like a cat." He shook another cake from the carton and ate it. "Come on, Eck," he said. "Start her off. How about ten dollars for that horse, Eck?"

"What need I got for a horse I would need a bear-trap to catch?" Eck said.

"Didn't you just see me catch him?"

"I seen you," Eck said. "And I don't want nothing as big as a horse if I got to wrastle with it every time it finds me on the same side of a fence it's on."[16]

Faulkner's description of the ponies is faintly reminiscent of Longstreet's "Horse-Swap," from which I quoted earlier. His horsetraders and Faulkner's Texas auctioneer, in their boasting, their self-assertive know-how, and their confidence in their ability to get rid of worthless horseflesh by their own rhetorical powers are much the same. So a genuine continuity can be observed. Yet how different are the authors' strategies of presentation.

Here I want to stress the continuity, and particularly the linguistic resources that both authors have to hand: they both have a language that is concrete, colorful, and yet in its own way very precise and even technical. At this point some of you may want to raise a question: Is it the language—this Southern language that I have been talking about—that gives them their great advantage? Or is it not rather the rich material that is available to both—that is to say, character types, dramatic settings, attitudes toward, and perceptions of, the kind of world that they live in?

It is a proper question and in my next lecture I shall try to address it. Yet in closing, let me ask you a question of my own. Is it possible to make a sharp distinction between the content and the form, between the personality of the Texas auctioneer and the language that he uses? Are not our attitudes toward people and events in great part shaped by the very language in which we describe them? When we try to describe one person to another or to a group, what do we say? Not usually how or what that person ate, rarely what he wore, only occasionally how he managed his job—no, what we tell is *what he said* and, if we are good mimics, *how he said it*. We apparently consider a person's spoken words the true essence of his being.

THREE

The Language in the Present Day

All true art is provincial, . . . of the very time and place of its making, out of human beings who are so particularly limited by their situation.
—Katherine Anne Porter, *The Days Before*

IT OCCURS TO ME THAT A POINT MADE IN MY LAST LECTURE may need further illustration, namely, my assertion that "the strength of even the most formal Southern writers stems from their knowledge of, and rapport with, the language spoken by the unlettered." It is an observation made again and again by modern literary critics. Nevertheless, an illustration may be useful.

In Robert Penn Warren's remarkable poem "Dragon Country," a real live dragon, with full equipment, including enormous leathern wings enabling it to take off vertically like a helicopter, has started raising hell in the state of Kentucky. Nobody in our day, including the most provincial Kentuckian, believes in dragons. But then how account for what happened to Jack Simms's hog pen?

> [Some] said it must be a bear, after some had viewed
> the location,
> With fence rails, like matchwood splintered, and earth a
> bloody mire.
> But no bear had been seen in the county in fifty years,
> they knew.

It was something to say, merely that, for people
    compelled to explain
What, standing in natural daylight, they couldn't
    believe to be true.

Yet evidence like this continues to mount up. A countryman, walking in the woods, discovers a

                        . . . wagon turned on its side,
    Mules torn from trace chains, and you saw how the
        harness had burst.
    Spectators averted the face from the spot where the
        teamster had died.

Who is the teller of this story? His use of words like *spec-
tators* and *averted* marks him as a man of some education, with
a knowledge of the great world outside. But we sense almost
immediately that he grew up in the country, is thoroughly
familiar with the local idiom, and can give an authentic
report on the impact that this horror made on his neighbors.
Thus he is doubly articulate and a convincing reporter on
what occurred. He even uses the speech rhythms of the plain
people.

    But that was long back, in my youth, just the first of
        case after case.
    The great hunts fizzled. You followed the track of
        disrepair,
    Ruined fence, blood-smear, brush broken, but came in
        the end to a place
    With weed unbent and leaf calm—and nothing,
        nothing, was there.
    So what, in God's name, could men think when they
        couldn't bring to bay
    That belly-dragging, earth-evil, but found that it took to
        air?

> Thirty-thirty or buckshot might fail, but at least you
>   could say
> You had faced it—assuming, of course, that you had
>   survived the affair.[1]

Though I have no liking for science fiction, and long ago gave up gothic horror stories, I always believe in Warren's dragon for just as long as I can hear his chosen narrator telling me about it, because his voice carries authority. So much for an intimate mingling of literary phrasings and the regional colloquial. The latter provides the reinforcement that gives conviction to the whole dramatic utterance.

I wish that time allowed me to give more examples from the Southern poets. Two more will have to suffice, and may be sufficient to make my point. John Crowe Ransom is celebrated for his elegant and carefully managed archaisms—one of the few modern poets who used something like an artificial diction. Yet his "Spiel of the Three Mountebanks"[2] is a vitriolically ironic exposé of three hot gospelers in the Southern mode; and even in his lyrics Ransom could on occasion insert lines such as the following:

> Autumn days in our section
> Are the most used-up thing on earth
> (Or in the waters under the earth)
> Having no more color nor predilection
> Than cornstalks too wet for the fire.[3]

The final comparison is not only beautifully exact—form almost without content and that content sodden and worthless—but intensely local and Southern.

Allen Tate, for all his intellectuality and his concern for the great philosophical issues, could also write his intensely local "The Swimmers,"[4] and lines such as

Man, dull critter of enormous head,
What would he look at in the coiling sky?[5]

The substitution of "creature" would destroy the whole impact of the line.

Yet, in spite of what the poets have to tell us about their final dependence on the colloquial, I turn back to our fiction writers, and with good reason. They provide the most obvious instances of the literary artist's dependence upon the spoken language, and for my present purposes the obvious is the more useful.

The prose of Eudora Welty will furnish excellent further instances, and will reveal aspects of the language that I have not thus far touched upon. For example, in her wonderful story called "The Petrified Man," we meet and listen to Leota, the beautician. The small-town beauty shop, obviously the local trading post for gossip, has cheapened and coarsened Leota's mind and spirit, but her arrival from a country setting into town has not sapped the vitality of her country-bred language.

A three-year-old toddles up to the chair that holds Leota's customer, and Leota explains his presence. "Ain't Billy Boy a sight? Only three years old, and already just nuts about the beauty-parlor business."[6] When the customer remarks that she hasn't seen him on earlier visits, Leota explains: "He ain't been here before, that's how come. He belongs to Mrs. Pike. She got her a job but it was Fay's Millinery. He oughtn't to try on those ladies' hats, they come down over his eyes like I don't know what. They just looks ridiculous, that's what, an' of course he's gonna put 'em on; hats. They tole Mrs. Pike they didn't appreciate him hangin' around there. Here he couldn't hurt a thing."[7]

Miss Welty uses the normal spelling for *thing*, but of

course what Leota actually said was *thaing*. But perhaps she took it for granted that most of her Southern readers would pronounce it this way without any prompting.

In spite of the scruffiness and tittle-tattle of her professional life, Leota still retains her hold on a lively and expressive vernacular English. So does Edna Earle Ponder in that marvelous story, *The Ponder Heart*. Edna Earle too is a born talker. I find it fascinating to listen to her, and listen we must, for the story is one unbroken monologue.

As Edna Earle remarks to the auditor she has captured, "if you read you'll put your eyes out. Let's just talk,"[8] though whether the man temporarily stranded in her hotel ever gets a word in edgewise seems doubtful. Edna Earle is clearly a high priestess of the oral tradition, which still flourishes in the South and which underlies so much of our written literature.

One reviewer has complained of the many clichés and trite expressions that the characters of Eudora Welty employ, remarking that their presence reflects "unimaginative thinking and [a] distrust of the new." To give examples, Edna Earle rattles off

glib comparisons such as "she was shallow as they come," she was as "pretty as a doll," "he ate me out of house and home," "good as gold," could "cut your hair to a fare-ye-well," "didn't bother her one whit," and so on. Well, of course Edna Earle uses such well-worn phrases, but all oral art makes use of such formulas and couldn't proceed without them. The English and Scottish folk ballads are filled with such conventional phrases, and even Homer in his *Iliad* uses over and over again such formulas as "the rosy-fingered dawn" and "the fleet-footed Achilles."

Another critic may ask: "Don't her people often use literary words that are quite out of character with their usual vocabulary?" For example, Edna Earle Ponder conjectures that "Maybe anybody's heart would *quail,* trying to keep up with Uncle Daniel's." Jack Renfro asks his father, "What brought you forth?" and tells Judge and Mrs. Judge Moody that "Banner is still my realm." How did these bookish terms, *quail* and *realm,* not to mention *brought forth,* get into the folk speech? Easy as pie, as Edna Earle would say. Right out of the King James Version of the Bible, or out of the hymns sung every Sunday morning in the Methodist and Baptist churches. If we need a reminder of the latter source, Miss Welty makes verses from the popular evangelical hymns resound again and again through the pages of *Losing Battles.*[9]

That novel provides a full display of her intimate knowledge of the folk idiom. As in *The Ponder Heart,* she skillfully uses it for comic entertainment, but she also finds in it a proper medium for depicting serious human concerns—for the expression of tenderness, pathos, and love.

One must point out that language of the folk is only one of Miss Welty's resources. For example, in *The Optimist's Daughter* she gives us characters in an urban setting and of a wholly different social stratum from those of *Losing Battles.* Yet in their conversation Laurel and her bridesmaids of an earlier year are unmistakably Southern. Attend to their conversation, and the reader will quickly sense that it could not emanate from a group of women living in a small midwestern town or from such a group in, say, Guilford, Connecticut.

Such characters as these are living in the fifties, sixties, and seventies of our century. So are most of those who people the short stories of Peter Taylor. His characters usually live in the upper South in cities such as Memphis or Nashville, or in the small county-seat towns of Tennessee. Many are fairly recently urbanized country people. Even those who live in the cities usually have kinsfolk still living out in the country. His South, then, is the midcentury South, now in transition, with new modes of living confronting the old-fashioned ways.

Taylor's "Miss Leonora When Last Seen" has to do with this transition. Miss Leonora is the last survivor of an aristocratic family that dominated the little town of Thomasville. She has high standards and would like to elevate the culture of the town. But she is no snob. For years she has been a schoolteacher, and she takes her pupils seriously— too seriously, many of them think.

The man who tells the story and who now owns and manages the local hotel was one of her pupils. He has resented her efforts to "make something" out of him and his fellows, and yet, almost in spite of himself, he admires her integrity, her belief in her ideals, and her disregard for adverse public opinion.

The town is going to be forced to integrate its schools. A hedge against this might be to zone off the town into two school districts, essentially white and black. But Miss Leonora's family home stands in the way. Though she lives well within the white district, there is a little cluster of black people living on her property, descendants of the family's former slaves.

Finally the decision is made to have her property condemned. This is a drastic step, but even the embittered town fathers retain some sense of civility. As the narrator puts it to us, his readers: "*Somebody* had to break the news to her. They couldn't just send the clerk up there with the notice, or, worse still, let her read it in the newspaper. The old lady had to be warned of how matters had gone."[10]

But the committee dreads the task, and when our narrator volunteers to go alone to deliver the news, the others cheerfully accept. When he arrives at Miss Leonora's, she has transformed herself.

She had done an awful thing to her hair. Her splendid white
mane, with its faded yellow streaks and its look of being kept up
on her head only by the two tortoise-shell combs at the back, was
no more. She had cut it off, thinned it, and set it in little waves
close to her head, and, worse still, she must have washed it in a
solution of indigo bluing. She had powdered the shine off her
nose, seemed almost to have powdered its sharpness and longness
away. She may have applied a little rouge and lipstick, though
hardly enough to be noticeable, only enough to make you realize
it wasn't the natural coloring of an old lady and enough to make
you *think* how old she was. And the dress she had on was exactly
right with the hair and the face, though at first I couldn't tell
why. . . .

Then it came to me. All that was lacking was a pair of pixie
glasses with rhinestone rims, and a half dozen bracelets on her
wrists. She was one of those old women who come out here from
Memphis looking for antiques and country hams and who tell
you how delighted they are to find a southern town that is truly
unchanged.[11]

Yet Miss Leonora, though she has disguised herself, sure-
ly has done so not in capitulation but in defiance, for she is
preparing to get into her car and drive away so that the writ
cannot be served on her, and Miss Leonora shows in her
first words of greeting that she remains her old self.

"I've felt so bad about your having to come here like this. I
knew they would put it off on you. Even you must have dreaded
coming, and you must hate me for putting you in such a position."

"Why, no. I wanted to come, Miss Leonora," I lied. "And I
hope you have understood that I had no part in the proceed-
ings. . . . "

"I do understand that," she said. "And we don't even need to
talk about any of it."[12]

And so, as in the past, Miss Leonora serves the mes-
senger of doom hot coffee and her little butter cookies. The

two exchange a bit more talk about the old days, and then our narrator finds himself actually putting Miss Leonora into her car and indeed—as he must have sensed—actually abetting her escape.

All this seems to me thoroughly Southern: the mutual unspoken understanding, the little courtesies, the façade of civility under almost any circumstances. But in conveying these niceties of the regional character, the language plays an essential part. The story is also, if one chooses to look at it so, a kind of parable of the ways in which a new South, with quite mixed emotions, bids farewell to an older South. But one notes that the character of the language survives the transition.

Peter Taylor employs his language for much the same delicate effects in many of his stories. His short story "Guests" will provide an apt illustration. Edward and Henrietta Harper have prevailed upon two of their country cousins to come to the city to pay them a visit. They believe that Cousin Johnny and his wife, Cousin Annie, ought to see the sights of Nashville. But Annie, though from the country, is thoroughly sensitive to condescension of any sort, and she doesn't fancy hearing her husband addressed as Cousin Johnny. Listen carefully to the following passage. It sounds unmistakably Southern to me.

"You mustn't think," she said, "that Mr. Kincaid and I can't dine at whatever your accustomed dinner hour is." This was very much in her usual vein—making known her awareness that they were dining earlier than was normal for the Harpers. Since the houseboy was removing the soup bowls at the time, it might have been supposed that what she said was meant for his ears and that she had phrased it with that in mind. But the old lady wasn't long in finding another occasion to refer to Cousin Johnny as "Mr. Kincaid." She did it a third and fourth time, even. Each time it was as if she feared they hadn't understood her before. Finally, though, she made it absolutely clear. During the meat course, while everyone except Cousin Johnny was working away at the roast lamb and baked potatoes, she drove the point home to her own satisfaction. "It isn't that Mr. Kincaid doesn't like roast lamb," she said, addressing herself to Edmund and speaking in the most old-fashioned country-genteel voice that Edmund had heard since he was a boy at home. "It isn't that he doesn't like roast lamb," she repeated. "It's that he dined alone with ladies at noon and so had to eat the greater share of an uncommonly fine cut of sirloin steak. He isn't, you understand, used to eating a great deal of meat." Now she turned to Henrietta. "He seldom eats any meat at all for supper." Edmund, remembering the other country ladies who had sat where Cousin Annie now sat, supposed that she would continue endlessly on this fascinating subject. But once she saw that she had the attention of both host and hostess, she suddenly turned to Cousin Johnny and said genially, "You seldom eat any meat at all for supper, do you, Mr. Kincaid?" It was the voice of a woman from an earlier generation than the Harpers', addressing her husband with the respect due a husband. How could anyone call him just plain Johnny after that?[13]

This passage is carefully, even elegantly, written, but the elegance is not that of Edith Wharton or of Henry James.

The work of Flannery O'Connor will provide more obvious examples of the Southern language as it was still used in the middle of our present century. Miss O'Connor's use of the language comes into the following passage by Robert Kiely, writing in the *New York Times Book Review*. There he comments upon the characters in a collection of stories by Joyce Carol Oates, and quotes from them such sample passages as the following:

"You said you'd help me with algebra sometime. . . . Then you forgot."

"I didn't forget."

"You don't like me. You've been avoiding me. . . . You come all the way here . . . to avoid me."

". . . I haven't been avoiding you; don't be ridiculous."

"You're ridiculous," she said, *unsmiling*.[14]

Kiely observes:

All such speeches in Miss Oates's collection are delivered without a smile. . . . One of the characteristics of these tired people and their worn-out language is the lack of the resilience necessary to express self-knowledge through humor.

Kiely continues:

The loss of accent and of wit signals a broader, more inclusive poverty. . . . [The characters in these stories] are, for the most part, creatures without will and therefore with very little of what normally passes for character. They do not choose one action instead of another any more than they choose one word rather than another. They are collections of compulsions, driven to behave in crude, destructive fashion while mouthing futile cliché after cliché.

Then Mr. Kiely makes another interesting observation. He writes: "Miss Oates has sometimes been compared to Flannery O'Connor," and he goes on to say: "If you take away the dialect, the laughter and the redemption, that's right. She's just like Flannery O'Connor."

Few of us will miss the irony of Kiely's final agreement. Take from any story its language, let alone characteristics like laughter and redemption, and you have stripped that story down to its bare bones. You have removed not merely its soul but its flesh and blood.

It is language, then, that both he and I want to stress, for it is through his language that the writer generates the laughter and the sense of proportion and perspective that render his characters credible human beings and not mere verbal scarecrows.

Miss O'Connor's stories abound in apt examples of expressive language. I choose the following from a story entitled "The Enduring Chill." As in a number of her later stories, the principal character, Asbury Fox, has broken away from the prejudices and general parochialism of his native South and has gone North to achieve for himself a freer and ampler life. In "The Enduring Chill" he has left his Georgia home for New York to achieve literary fame. As a writer he has failed, and knows it. He has become not only depressed but physically ill, and now he has come home to die.

The impulse of his good-hearted and practical mother is to call in the family doctor, but Asbury has the same contempt for small-town medicine as he has for small-town Southern culture. When Dr. Brock does arrive, Asbury treats him with scant courtesy, and Mrs. Fox feels it necessary to apologize. Her son "wouldn't act so ugly if he weren't really sick. And I want you," she tells the doctor, "to come back every day until you get him well." The expressions "act so ugly" and "get him well" strike me as pure Southern and are certainly familiar.

Mrs. Fox owns a small dairy—in which her son had scorned to work—and employs two very competent young black men, Randall and Morgan, to tend the cows and manage the milking machines. Before Asbury had gone to New York he had one day out in the dairy picked up a jelly glass from which the Negroes drank water and poured himself a glass of milk. Randall tells him, "She don't 'low that. . . . That *the* thing she don't 'low."[15] But Asbury replies, "Listen . . . the world is changing. There's no reason I shouldn't drink after you or you after me." Randall explains: "She don't 'low noner us to drink this here milk."

Asbury persists. "Take the milk, it's not going to hurt my mother to lose two or three glasses of milk a day. We've got to think free if we want to live free." Morgan remarks, "I ain't seen you drink none of it yourself." Asbury actually despises milk and is drinking it, and urging Randall and Morgan to drink it, as a gesture of defiance against what he considers his mother's too-bossy ways.

Asbury asks Morgan, "Don't you like milk?" Morgan answers, "I likes it but I ain't drinking noner that." "Why?" "She don't 'low it."[16]

A few days later Asbury overhears Morgan asking, "How come you let him drink all that milk every day?" "What he do is him," Randall answers. "What I do is me." "How come he talk so ugly about his ma?" "She didn't whup him enough when he was little," Randall said.[17]

Asbury, convinced that he is about to die and determined to do so as a doomed, failed, romantic artist, asks his mother to call Randall and Morgan to his bedside so that he may bid them farewell. They arrive and again Asbury has put them in a completely false position. Their necessarily awkward attempts to handle the situation claim our sympathies.

The two of them came in grinning and shuffled to the side of the bed. They stood there, Randall in front and Morgan behind. "You sho do look well," Randall said. "You looks very well."

"You looks well," the other one said. "Yessuh, you looks fine."

"I ain't ever seen you looking so well before," Randall said.

"Yes, doesn't he look well?" his mother said. "I think he looks just fine."

"Yessuh," Randall said. "I speck you ain't even sick."

"Mother," Asbury said in a forced voice, "I'd like to talk to them alone."[18]

Mrs. Fox, though obviously offended, walks out of the room, leaving, to their dismay, Randall and Morgan to cope with the situation as best they can.

Asbury's head was so heavy he could not think what he had been going to do. "I'm dying," he said.

Both their grins became gelid. "You looks fine," Randall said.

"I'm going to die," Asbury repeated. Then with relief he remembered that they were going to smoke together. He reached for the package on the table and held it out to Randall, forgetting to shake out the cigarettes.

The Negro took the package and put it in his pocket. "I thank you," he said. "I certainly do prechate it."

Asbury stared as if he had forgotten again. After a second he became aware that the other Negro's face had turned infinitely sad; then he realized that it was not sad but sullen. He fumbled in the drawer of the table and pulled out an unopened package and thrust it at Morgan.

"I thanks you, Mist Asbury," Morgan said, brightening.

"You certly does look well."

"I'm about to die," Asbury said irritably.

"You looks fine," Randall said. . . .

"I speck you might have a little cold," Randall said after a time.

"I takes a little turpentine and sugar when I has a cold," Morgan said.[19]

A little later old Dr. Brock comes in with the proper diagnosis. He had taken a blood sample from Asbury's arm, telling him, "Blood don't lie," and has found that Asbury is suffering from brucellosis or undulant fever, evidently contracted last year, before he left for New York, as the result of his having foolishly and mischievously insisted on drinking unpasteurized milk to spite his mother. His ailment, far from being the mysteriously romantic affliction that Asbury had supposed it to be, is physical, diagnosable, and eventually curable. Asbury is not going to die of it.

I have not been fair to the story in my failing to deal with it as a whole, but my obvious concern here is with Miss O'Connor's brilliant handling of the language, and particularly of "the country idiom" which Robert Fitzgerald tells us she so much loved.

Flannery O'Connor's stories bring us down into mid-century. So does the work of Walker Percy, even into the third quarter of our century. In his work I find the Southern language—always fitted and adjusted to his own fictional purposes—alive, well, and vigorous.

Percy's range of types of character is wide: included are modern New Orleanians, representatives of the old Delta plantation stock, and black Southerners of all sorts, including the college-bred professional of the present day.

The aunt of Binx Bolling, the protagonist of *The Moviegoer*, is a patrician lady, which statement must not be taken to imply that she lacks a certain pungency of style. In the passage to be quoted she is berating Binx for his misconduct. According to her standards (and to a great degree, Binx's own) he has acted badly. He has done much worse than offend her; she believes he has disgraced his upbringing.

"Were you intimate with Kate?"
"Intimate?"
"Yes."
"Not very."
"I ask you again. Were you intimate with her?"
"I suppose so. Though intimate is not quite the word."
"You suppose so. Intimate is not quite the word. I wonder

what is the word. You see . . . there is another of my hidden assumptions. All these years I have been assuming that between us words mean roughly the same thing, that among certain people, gentlefolk I don't mind calling them, there exists a set of meanings held in common, that a certain manner and a certain grace come as naturally as breathing. At the great moments of life—success, failure, marriage, death—our kind of folks have always possessed a native instinct for behavior, a natural piety or grace, I don't mind calling it. . . . Oh I am aware that we hear a great many flattering things nowadays about your great common man—you know it has always been revealing to me that he is perfectly content so to be called, because that is exactly what he is: the common man and when I say common I mean common as hell. . . . [She looks out the window at a passerby.] They say out there we think we're better. You're damn right we're better. . . . Perhaps we are a biological sport. . . . But one thing I am sure of: we live by our lights, we die by our lights, and whoever the high gods may be, we'll look them in the eye without apology."[20]

I must interrupt the lady here, for my time is limited, but her tirade goes on for two pages.

My next quotation is not so much a sample of twentieth-century Southern speech as a description of the manners and conversational maneuvers that regulate Southern conversation. Bill Barrett, of *The Last Gentleman,* is here meeting for the first time Mr. and Mrs. Vaught of Alabama. They meet in a New York hospital room where the Vaughts have brought their son for treatment.

"Where're you from," cried Mrs. Vaught in a mock-accusatory tone he recognized and knew how to respond to.

"Ithaca," he said, smiling. "Over in the Delta." He felt himself molt. In the space of seconds he changed from a Southerner in the North, an amiable person who wears the badge of his origin in a faint burlesque of itself, to a Southerner in the South, a skillful player of an old play who knows his cues and waits smiling in the wings. You stand in the posture of waiting on ladies and when one of them speaks to you so, with mock-boldness and mock-anger (and a bit of steel in it too), you knew how to take it. They were onto the same game. Mrs. Vaught feasted her eyes on him. He was *nice*. (She, he saw at once, belonged to an older clan than Mr. Vaught; she knew ancient cues he never heard of.) She could have married him on the spot and known what she was getting.[21]

Later, when young Mr. Barrett returns to the South, he suffers a kind of cultural shock. Percy's description of it represents him at his ironic best—yet there is a vein of seriousness too.

The South he came home to was different from the South he had left. It was happy, victorious, Christian, rich, patriotic and Republican.

The happiness and serenity of the South disconcerted him. He had felt good in the North because everyone else felt so bad. True, there was a happiness in the North. That is to say, nearly everyone would have denied that he was unhappy. And certainly the North was victorious. It had never lost a war. But Northerners had turned morose in their victory. They were solitary and shut-off to themselves and he, the engineer, had got used to living among them. Their cities, rich and busy as they were, nevertheless looked bombed out. And his own happiness had come from being onto the unhappiness beneath their happiness. It was possible for him to be at home in the North because the North was homeless. There are many things worse than being homeless in a homeless place—in fact, this is one condition of being at home, if you are yourself homeless. For example, it is much worse to be homeless and then to go home where everyone is at home and then still be homeless. The South was at home. Therefore his homelessness was much worse in the South because he had expected to find himself at home there.

The happiness of the South was very formidable. It was an almost invincible happiness. It defied you to call it anything else. Everyone was in fact happy. The women were beautiful and charming. The men were healthy and successful and funny; they knew how to tell stories. They had everything the North had and more. They had a history, they had a place redolent with memories, they had good conversation, they believed in God and defended the Constitution, and they were getting rich in the bargain. They had the best of victory and defeat. Their happiness was aggressive and irresistible. He was determined to be as happy as anyone, even though his happiness before had come from Northern unhappiness. If folks down here are happy and at home, he told himself, then I shall be happy and at home too.[22]

In Percy's *Lancelot* the narrator, Lancelot Lamar, has helped a very talented young black man, Elgin Buell, to achieve an education. He says of Elgin,

It was as if he had sailed in a single jump from Louisiana pickaninny playing marbles under a chinaberry tree to a smart-ass M.I.T. senior, leapfrogging not only the entire South but all of history as well. And maybe he knew what he was doing. From cotton patch to quantum physics and glad not to have stopped along the way.

But he and his family had yet another reason to be grateful to me, a slightly bogus reason, to be sure, which I in my own slightly bogus-liberal fashion was content not to have set straight. He thought I saved his family from the Klan. In a way I did. . . . It was true I went to see the Grand Kleagle and the harassment stopped. The story which I never had quite the energy or desire to correct was that in the grand mythic Lamar tradition I had confronted the Kleagle in his den, "called him out" with some such Southern Western shoot-out ultimatum as "Now listen here, you son of a bitch, I don't know which one of you is bothering Ellis [Buell] but I'm holding you responsible and if one hair of a Buell head is harmed, I'm going to shoot your ass off for you," and so forth and so forth. I put a stop to it all right, but in a manner more suited to Southern complexities and realities than the simple dreams of the sixties, when there were only good people and bad people. I went to see the Grand Kleagle all right, who was none

other than J.B. Jenkins, a big dumb boy who played offensive tackle
with me in both high school and college. . . . He was a good family
man, believed in Jesus Christ, America, the Southern way of life,
hated Communists and liberals, and was not altogether wrong on
any count. At any rate, all I said to him was "Now, J.B., I want you
to do me a favor." "What's that, Lance, old buddy?" "You know
what I want. I want you to lay off Ellis and his church." . . . [J.B.
protests, but Lamar asks him,] "Will you take my word for something, J.B.?" "You know I will." "I swear to you that Ellis is a good
God-fearing Baptist like you and you have nothing to fear from
him. . . . He's been working for us for forty years and you know
that." "Well, that's true. Well, all right, Lance. Don't worry about
nothing. Les us have a drink." . . . And that was that.[23]

The foregoing quotations constitute only a small and
scattered sampling from Southern literature. Think of the
names that I have wholly omitted: Mary Boykin Chesnut,
William Gilmore Simms, Kate Chopin, Ellen Glasgow,
Caroline Gordon, Andrew Lytle, Katherine Anne Porter,
Reynolds Price, Carson McCullers, Ralph Ellison, Ernest
Gaines, A. R. Ammons, James Dickey, Beth Henley, to
name only a few. Our youngest generation is omitted almost
entirely.

I can only hope that the passages I have cited are sufficient to make my point: namely, that a Southern language
veritably exists and constitutes a rich resource for the writers of the South.

Obviously, the presence of even a rich and vital language
will not make up for a user's lack of sensibility, intelligence,
and imagination. The dull and awkward writer will remain
so, with even the language of Shakespeare at his disposal.
Nevertheless, a rich and expressive language counts for a
great deal.

What is the future of the language of the South? Can it be

said to have a future? In an increasingly urban, mobile, and industrialized society, can it survive? I'm not sure, but I have heard its death prophesied so often—as early as the 1920s with the advent of radio—that I have begun to take heart. It clearly has staying power.

I am confident, however, that I can identify its most dangerous enemy. It is not education properly understood, but miseducation: foolishly incorrect theories of what constitutes good English, an insistence on spelling pronunciations, and the propagation of bureaucratese, sociologese, and psychologese, which American business, politics, and academies seem to exude as a matter of course. The grave faults are not the occasional use of *ain't* but the bastard concoctions from a Latinized vocabulary produced by people who never studied Latin. Gobbledygook is a waste of everybody's time.

The great poet of our century, William Butler Yeats, years ago faced the problem as it manifested itself in Ireland. He rejoiced in the unwritten literature of the folk: the ballad, the folk song, and the folk tale. They were genuine art, and required no apology to anybody. He also revered the great tradition of written literature that has behind it Sophocles, Dante, and Shakespeare. The two literatures did not compete, but complemented each other.[24]

Like Yeats's Ireland, the South has had a vigorous oral literature and, like Ireland again, a brilliant written literature, particularly in our present century. The great danger, as Yeats saw it, was that the mass of people would lose the virtues of the unwritten tradition without ever having achieved mastery of the great written tradition. They would thus be doubly losers: to have lost the ability to tell a good yarn or appreciate it when told, and yet not be able to read with understanding and delight the great literature of the past and present. Such loss is not made up for by sitting bemused, watching a situation comedy or even the best programs of our public television networks for four or five hours a day. If such losers do read at all, it's more often predigested fare that comes off the stands of the drugstore, not the shelves of a library or an honest-to-goodness bookstore.

Genuine literature is not a luxury commodity but neither is it an assembly-line product. It cannot be mass produced. It has to be hand made, fashioned by a genuine craftsman out of honest human emotions and experiences, in the making of which the indispensable material is our common language, in all its variety, complexity, and richness. Otherwise the literary craftsman has no way of expressing whatever penetrating insights into the human predicament he may possess—no way of setting forth for others his passionate feeling, his wit, or his wisdom.

Notes

ONE
Where It Came From

1. Richard N. Current, *Northernizing the South* (Athens: University of Georgia Press, 1983), p. 2.
2. *The Portable James Joyce,* ed. Harry Levin (New York: Viking, 1947), p. 452.
3. E. J. Dobson, *English Pronunciation, 1500–1700,* 2 vols. (Oxford: Clarendon Press, 1968), vol. 2, secs. 41 and 42.
4. Eilert Ekwall, *Historische neuenglische Laut-und Formeniehre* (Berlin and Leipzig, 1922), sec. 42.
5. George Philip Krapp, *The English Language in America,* 2 vols. (New York: Frederik Ungar, 1925), 2:237.
6. Helge Kökeritz, *The Phonology of the Suffolk Dialect* (Uppsala, 1932), pp. 3–7.
7. "Position of the Charleston Dialect," *Publications of the American Dialect Society* 22 (April 1955): 37.
8. Joseph Wright, *English Dialect Grammar* (Oxford, 1903), sec. 121.
9. Ibid., sec. 210.
10. Mark Antony Lower, *The Song of Solomon: The Dialect of Sussex* (London, 1860).
11. Krapp, *The English Language in America,* 2:226.
12. Dobson, *English Pronunciation,* 1:105.
13. John Aubrey, *Brief Lives,* ed. Andrew Clark (Oxford: Clarendon Press, 1898), 2:182.
14. W. D. Parish, "A Dictionary of the Kentish Dialect," Publications of the English Dialect Society, no. 20 (1887), p. vi; Alexander J. Ellis, *On Early English Pronunciation* (London, 1889), p.

1563; and Joseph Wright, *The English Dialect Grammar* (Oxford, 1905), sec. 311.

15. *The Survey of English Dialects*, pt. B, *The Basic Materials*, ed. Harold Orton and Martyn F. Wakelin (Leeds: University of Leeds, 1968), vol. 4, pt. 3, 9.10.1, 2, and 3.

16. "A Word List from East Alabama," *Dialect Notes* 3, no. 2 (1908): 279–328, 3, no. 5 (1909): 343–91.

17. "The Phonology of the Uncle Remus Stories," *Publications of the American Dialect Society*, no. 22 (November 1954), pp. 3–59. See also his "Dialect Differentiation in the Stories of Joel Chandler Harris," *American Literature* 27 (March 1958): 88–96

18. See "African Jack," in *Nights with Uncle Remus*, and other African (or Daddy) Jack stories in this collection (Boston and New York: Houghton Mifflin, 1881), p. 134 and passim. See also the introduction, pp. xxviii–xxxv, for Harris's discussion of the differences between the Gullah dialect and that spoken by Uncle Remus. This introduction is omitted from the convenient *Complete Tales of Uncle Remus* (Boston: Houghton Mifflin, 1955).

19. The southwest counties also show strong affinities with our Coastal Southern dialect. See my *Relation of the Alabama-Georgia Dialect to the Provincial Dialects of Great Britain* (Baton Rouge: Louisiana State University Press, 1935).

20. W. D. Parish, "A Dictionary of the Sussex Dialect," *English Dialect Society* 6, no. 2 (1875): 6.

TWO
The Language of the Gentry and the Folk

1. *The Fathers and Other Fiction* (Baton Rouge: Louisiana State University Press, 1977), p. 17.

2. *Georgia Scenes . . . by a Native Georgian*, 2d ed. (New York: Harper and Brothers, 1875), pp. 24–25.

3. Ibid., p. 29.

4. *The Complete Tales of Uncle Remus*, comp. Richard Chase (Boston: Houghton Mifflin, 1955), p. 488.

5. Ibid., p. 491. The adjective *soon* requires comment. The *OED* does give instances of its adjectival use as here, meaning an

early or speedy event or happening. So does the *English Dialect Dictionary.* But neither cites an application to the quickness of intellect of an individual. Such is, of course, not too difficult a transition. It may have been made by the American black people.

6. Ibid., p. 493.

7. Ibid., p. 494.

8. *The Fathers*, pp. 267–68.

9. Robert Penn Warren, *All the King's Men* (New York: Harcourt Brace, 1946), pp. 175–76.

10. Ibid., p. 155.

11. Robert Penn Warren, *At Heaven's Gate* (New York: Harcourt Brace, 1943), p. 119.

12. William Faulkner, *Go Down, Moses* (New York: Random House, Vintage Books, 1973), pp. 140–41.

13. Ibid., p. 141.

14. William Faulkner, *The Hamlet* (New York: Random House, Vintage Books, 1956), p. 307.

15. Ibid., p. 285.

16. Ibid., p. 289.

THREE
The Language in the Present Day

1. Robert Penn Warren, *Selected Poems, 1923–1975* (New York: Random House, 1976), pp. 253–54.

2. John Crowe Ransom, *Poems and Essays* (New York: Random House, Vintage Books, 1955), pp. 17–19.

3. Ibid., p. 23.

4. Allen Tate, *Poems* (Denver: Swallow Press, 1961), pp. 175–79.

5. Ibid., p. 50.

6. Eudora Welty, *A Curtain of Green* (Garden City, N.Y.: Doubleday, 1941), p. 32.

7. Ibid., p. 37.

8. Eudora Welty, *The Ponder Heart* (New York: Harcourt, Brace, 1954), p. 11.

9. Cleanth Brooks, "Eudora Welty and the Southern Idiom," in *Eudora Welty: A Form of Thanks*, ed. Ann J. Abadie and Louis D.

Dollarhide (Jackson: University Press of Mississippi, 1979), pp. 15–16.

10. Peter Taylor, *Miss Leonora When Last Seen and Fifteen Other Stories* (New York: Obolensky, 1968), p. 269.

11. Ibid., pp. 274–75.

12. Ibid., p. 275.

13. Peter Taylor, *Happy Families Are All Alike* (Philadelphia: Lippincott, 1962), pp. 181–82.

14. In the *New York Times Book Review* for January 6, 1981. The passages quoted from Kiely occur on pp. 1 and 21. The book reviewed was *A Sentimental Education* (New York: Dutton, 1981).

15. Flannery O'Connor, *Everything That Rises Must Converge* (New York: Noonday Press, 1965), p. 97.

16. Ibid., p. 98.

17. Ibid., p. 98.

18. Ibid., p. 110.

19. Ibid., pp. 110–11.

20. Walker Percy, *The Moviegoer* (New York: Knopf, 1961), pp. 222–24.

21. Walker Percy, *The Last Gentleman* (New York: Farrar, Straus, and Giroux, 1966), p. 52.

22. Ibid., pp. 177–78.

23. Walker Percy, *Lancelot* (New York: Farrar, Straus, and Giroux, 1977), p. 92–93.

24. William Butler Yeats, *Essays and Introductions* (New York: Macmillan, 1961), pp. 3–12.